D0922011

Readiness

Readiness

Prose Poems

Mark Cox

Press 53
Winston-Salem

Press 53, LLC
PO Box 30314
Winston-Salem, NC 27130

First Edition

Copyright © 2018 by Mark Cox

All rights reserved, including the right of reproduction in whole or in
part in any form except in the case of brief quotations embodied in
critical articles or reviews. For permission, contact publisher at
editor@Press53.com, or at the address above.

Cover design by Kevin Morgan Watson

Cover photograph, "170A6128 Fading Echoes," Copyright © 2016
by Jen Johnson, used by permission of the artist.
jenjohnson.com

Author photo by Nancy Card

Library of Congress Control Number
2018933566

Printed on acid-free paper
ISBN 978-1-941209-78-3

For Jack Myers
(1941 − 2009)

The author thanks the editors of the following venues, in which these poems first appeared:

Blackbird: "Chutes and Ladders," "Here," "The Storm-Torn Edge of Heaven"

Chautauqua: "Wrought"

Conte Online: "Four Coasts"

Crazyhorse: "I Love You, Boy"

Dog Music: An Anthology of Poems about Dogs: "The Present" (formerly "History")

The Florida Review: "Focus," "Knossos"

Green Mountains Review: "The Late Show," "Readiness"

The Lightning Key Review: "Ladder on the Ground"

Miramar: "History," "Home," "The Journey to and from Is Neither"

New Ohio Review: "No Picnic in the Afterlife"

Numéro Cinq: "Balls," "Headstrong," "Level," "Prisoners," "Suncatchers"

Open to Interpretation—Intimate Landscape: "Beauty, 1976"

Pinyon: "Cathedral"

Sou'wester: "The Hitching Post"

Contents

There is special providence in the fall of a sparrow. If it be now, 'tis not to come; if it be not to come, it will be now; if it be not now, yet it will come. The readiness is all.

—William Shakespeare

After I've winnowed the poems, the wind will seem to have blown the seeds right out of oblivion. But it is only taking life from life, the many from the one, which is how I came to be and is what I have done.

—Jack Myers

I. The Springs

No Picnic in the Afterlife

When I'm feeling down about the human condition, that is, *my* human condition, I consider all the crappy jobs I could have suffered in another life. An executioner, say, or worse, the lucky schmuck to cart the bodies away—there are more difficult trials than poetry, aren't there, I remind myself. What if I'd been a mummy maker, with a desiccation degree, that would be no cakewalk; mummification was an industry, processing thousands of ibises and sacred cats—bulls even (those whoppers took forty days in high sun to dry) and speaking of meat, sacred or no, the smell was awful (those long shifts under blood orange Egyptian suns, you never got used to it, when you went home your wife refused to make love with you). But it was an important job, this populating the afterlives of others, providing guard creatures and pets, not to mention the colossal stores of foodstuffs, none of which could you sneak home, the guards always patting you down; Ra forbid your old lady should be grateful enough to give an inch or you should live even a minute of the afterlife you made for others. No, it is your lot to cater that picnic in paradise, never to partake of it, you have to be committed, as I tell my students, it is a way of life. The priests, they handled the people, they didn't really get it, what it entails to mummify a goddamn bull or fifteen-foot crocodile—they were freaking huge—and the baboons, you had to yank their canines, housebreak them dentally, *before* putting them down. No, it is no small job to populate the afterlife, it takes a brutal tenderness, attention to life's cruel details, all that moisture by which we live, the very lubricant of our mobility, drawn out molecule by molecule (though we didn't think so micro then), and there you were lacing up your sandals, snagging some rice cakes and dates for lunch, leaving for work, which, though worse than poetry as fates go, could have been truly horrific—you could be quarrying stone for temples (lousy hours on barges, mosquitoes big as dung beetles, no hazard pay)—No, you had your own role to slave over, supplying pharaohs and courtesans a kind of Noah's ark of totems and sacrifices, right down to the royal cock fights, so who could blame you for amusing yourself with the occasional mummy joke—the kitten placed in the sarcophagus of a lion, an ibis nested in a crocodile, a fish inside the ibis, a scarab inside the fish. It got you through those long ass days while the sweat was sucked out of you gram by gram or iota by iota or however by whatever they measured it, and for what? What was waiting at dark? A woman who couldn't bear the stink of death on you, who probably spent most of her day rubbing olive oil into some noble's feet! And so you get home and heave yourself down onto a grass mat and say there just has to be a better way than this, than this life I am living, and your wife says quit your bitching, this once, this once I'll get the oil, and here you are, back in your hut of baked mud and palm thatching, your staff and sandals propped by the front door and it is cooler here out of the goddamn sun, out of history, a moment's pause, an eddy in the Nile, and it doesn't matter if your sweetheart has been anointing other men's feet or polishing their silver till her poor hands blackened, or the *Papyrus Monthly* won't publish your work—you are together now, in this life, in this moment and the napping baby has your nose and the over-pounded, unleavened, tooth-shattering bread is warm, so quit your whining, you could be humping pyramid blocks through sandstorms, you've got it good, you can barely smell yourself anymore, you are golden—here, have a fig.

Art

The little wren in the museum seems to have had quite enough culture and would like an open window now, thank you very much. He flits from century to century, gilded frame by frame. Here, the still life he vivifies with a splat. There, a foxhunt fraught with hounds and horses—he steers clear of that! Likewise, the storm-battered riggings of a besieged frigate and the onyx clutches of an Egyptian cat. He glides over the windmill and tulips, a haughty van Dyck; he banks past the tortured torso of a Cubist woman and comes to rest, finally, on a medieval pike. Ouch! But just wait till Dolores gets a load of this. Who's boring and has no taste for the finer things, now? She wants ambition? She wants a mate who soars? Those philistine pigeons on fake statues out front, they don't have a clue about the real art indoors. What a strange and solitary freedom. It's heady, such perspective, yet he hungers, nonetheless. Tonight, an expert will bait a trap with songbirds and seed. What happens then is anybody's guess.

The Seagull

Once, when my father was surfcasting in Florida, he caught a seagull. It remains unclear whether the gull was hungry or just happening by, but it made for a good story later about the quality of his lure; that, and the nut-sized brain behind our poor bird's terrified eyes. For half an hour, using needle-nose pliers and forceps, they worked to clear the treble hooks, but avoid damage to its bony wing. And surprisingly, the bird stayed pretty much completely still, as if it knew it had no other choice in this, surrounded and shaded by a flock of humans, plastered to the wet sand, at the mercy of some higher power. When my father at last unhanded him, he did not fly off right away. He bumbled to his feet and looked around, as if to verify he was truly free. For all he knew, he was still affixed to that invisible line, and forever more would be. He could flap all he wanted, but he wasn't going anywhere, so what was the point? Plus, it hurt, for Pete's sake; you make it only so far and—oopf!—get the hell torn out of you. In fact, it seemed for a while as if he might not fly off at all, that maybe he had reassessed his precious life while lying there on his back and was really going to do things differently from now on. No more crapping in flight, no more dumpster diving down at the Save-More, no more parking lot loitering. Just fresh crustaceans, long walks in tide pools, home to roost early with the missus. He was going to be a sand piper or something cutesy like that, not some rat with wings, as the crabbers called him—he was going to change his life. Then, he seemed to hear the other gulls squalling over chum out on the water. Someone stepped back and the blunt sun hit him square in his beady seabird eyes. And just like that, he was gone, lifting off as if nothing had ever held him there, returned within moments to his brothers, indistinguishable and content.

The Springs

The young people are gathered in the narrows of the river. They are like seals among the rocks, or like mermaids surrounding shipwrecked sailors, in varied poses of relaxation and leisure. The sun-struck water glints, but is icy to the touch; their six-packs cool in shallow pools among the stones. Now and again, one of the girls brushes her hair or adjusts some slight aspect of her appearance. It is an endless summer day. It is a brief summer. No one wants to go home empty handed, unfulfilled, though no one is quite sure what fulfillment means. The boys are muscular and lean, deeply tanned except for the strip the girls can see just between their shorts and underwear when they hug their knees. That flesh seems almost fluorescent. It's not that it is attractive. You just can't help thinking about it. The girls are wearing two-pieces, most with cut-offs. Everything about them reminds the boys of peaches.

Some feelings wait years to be loosed, to be finally written. I have retained this image for decades, unable to decode it. Nearing sixty, I still don't know what it means. I know the river rushes past on every side. I know the young people only seem to stay young forever. I understand that the beer warms and the bodies become flabby and the hearts weaken and grow weary of each other. The shy girl on the far left had a taxing life. She lost her husband and infant daughter to a car wreck and never remarried. The boy beside her stayed in town and worked on trucks and took to liquor on lonely weekends. But there would have been joy too, senses of elation at the school bus stop, promotions at the agency, confidences kept between the best of friends. There would have been a lifetime of moments at kitchen tables to come: strong coffee, the local paper, toast buttered with spoons because the dishwasher never got run.

But this is all, always, many years ahead. This day is bright and sharply defined, arrested, as if it were a sculpture in some European fountain commemorating youth and its vigor, that early season of our being. And so, these figures remain for me, ageless, a constant in my passing life and occasionally I go down to the river and stand by the lazy drift of water. I know better than to get in, but it is calming to watch from a distance as they sun themselves there—laughing, preening, teasing—touching one another in the small ways humans do.

Autumn Longings

The girls are restless down by the docks. The sunlight is waning and the water is darkening around the little pier. The lake pushes gently against the algae-coated wood, harder and more rhythmically as small boats come in. They know it is just a county lake, it is nothing like the ocean, but something about nightfall is unsettling. There is a depth to these waters that goes beyond how far a lure can sink to the bottom. There is something murky and inexplicable about it, something eerie about the mist that lolls over it on the unpredictable nights of this changing season. Sometimes they wade in the shallows where the silt is fine and won't abrade their tender feet. Sometimes they watch the men and boys come in off the water to clean their catch. The fish shine in the sun, struggling on their stringers, dripping lake water and blood, their gills still working in the open air. It is hard to look at it, but hard not to watch. There is something ancient in the ritual, the way the muscular boys hold up the fish just so for the girls to admire, measuring and weighing to judge who has caught the most impressive of the day. Back at the campsites, the mothers will cook these fish in clean oil for the evening's supper. The fish will have become something else entirely in a matter of hours. Raccoons will rustle through their heads and skeletons in the dumpsters. The lake will be black then, with a frosting of fog. The stars will spark in the sky as they have for billions of years. Light dew will accrue on the tents and trailers. The girls will sleep, uneasy in their goose down bags, their legs opening and closing a little, as if to swim or make love; their mouths moving, as if to kiss or chew. One way or the other, in the morning they will wake famished, hungry for anything but fish.

Level

Each evening when they stop at a campground, he helps his father level the trailer. Everything has to be just right. You want the water to flow correctly, don't you? You want the floors to be just like home and to wake up without a headache, don't you? They move from corner to corner, adjusting the jacks. The boy stares at the bubble in the level. He calls out when it centers itself. Everything is ready then. There is a calm when they fit the folding chairs in a semi-circle around the fire pit. They hang the gas lantern from a limb and lug the cooler onto the picnic table. Soon, there is the sun's glow against them all as it lowers beyond the trees. Now, his father can begin drinking in earnest and without pretense. Now, it is time for the night animals to stir. The strong can stalk and the weak must cower from hiding place to hiding place, feeding as quietly as possible. The boy knows how it looks to neighbors. A content family. Everything calculated just so. What did it matter? The leaves fell each autumn and were replaced. All the foliage here would be reduced to topsoil before he could even drive a car. The light would still stain blood red on trees at sundown. The dark was sure to come. There was nothing for him to do about it. He knows just two things for certain: he never wants to become like his father and he must control everything he can. It is just a matter of time. One day, he will have a family of his own and things will be done his way—his way and no one else's.

Headstrong

Their skeletons are still below the spillway. There is even some ravaged hide left, if one would call it that. Tough way to go, the boy thinks. The two goats even seem to be facing each other, just as they must have on the dam itself, barring each other's passage along the narrow walkway. Not quite halfway across is where it seems to have happened—they met here and could get no farther.

The boy toes a stone over and feels it in his stomach as it drops and strikes the earth. It hasn't rained much this summer, the crops are withering, the county reservoir is low. The spillway is as dry as—well, as dry as these bones, now uncovered and bleaching in the high sun.

Goats are gifted climbers; even plain old billies are nimble by nature. It would have been easy enough to pass. Or for one or both to turn and walk the other way. Headstrong, his mother calls it. She says it with a mixture of disdain and resignation, and just a touch of pride. She says he comes from a long line of stubborn men. Men, he knows, who get things done. Men who finish what they start. Men who make things happen, no matter what the cost. The boy knows that some people thrive on conflict. He has seen the aggressive kids get their way. Maybe people are just angry that life is brief. That's why they want everything now.

The boy kicks another stone over the spillway, then a bottle cap packed with parched dirt. It lands squarely between the two dead goats, their skulls still poised at one another. What does anyone really want? To have been understood in this world; to walk this spillway, the hallways of his school, the streets of his little town, and be acknowledged as having been. To be considered. To be reckoned with. To be taken into account. The boy stands at the middle till he can feel the skin raging on the back of his neck. Then he turns and goes back the way he came.

Balls

The boy's testicles hurt. This is a new thing. He straddles his bike gingerly, one foot still on a pedal, the other on the guardrail of the overpass. It is 10:30 in the morning. Traffic has lessened, but is steady on the interstate. It is the long-distance travelers now, not the commuters. It is the people who are really going places, seeing things he would like to see. A hundred years ago, he would be barefoot by a river, watching his cork bobber dip in the water, watching driftwood or the occasional barge make its way downstream. This tenderness, the internet says, is part of growing up. It has to do with need and physical change in the body. He can expect a bunch more where this came from.

If he times it right, he can spit onto the roofs of tractor-trailers. He doesn't know why this matters, that even a little of himself swept out of town is better than none at all. To him, it comes out more like contempt and just feels like the thing to do. He hesitates a long time before he starts tossing rocks, gravel at first, then larger, trying to see how much he can get away with. There's contact, but to his amazement it goes unnoticed, the world just speeds by; no one pulls over or lays on their horn. It is going to be a long summer. He could look for Jimmy and his pals, they always seem to bike around in a pack. Or he could head south and check out the new construction in that neighborhood next to school. He could snag a beer from the crew's coolers— anything with an element of risk. He can't go home yet; there is nothing there but chores he's been avoiding, help his single mother needs around the house.

Cars are still streaming beneath him. The spit on those trucks, it is in the next county already and he is still here on this overpass in the searing sun watching the world in its various glossy colors pass him by. None of it, none of it sets quite right with him. He squirms a bit to get comfortable and he tugs at the crotch of his jeans.

Voice

I don't remember how I got in, only that I was there, beneath the flooring, against the foundation of a half-constructed house. The masons were bricking it over and I was pretending, as light diminished, to be entombed forever, never again to be called in for dinner or out for a game of ball.

Today, this would be a lawsuit waiting to happen, but back then, in the mid-sixties, the workers played along, felt it was harmless and funny; I was just a ten-year-old with summer on my hands. What made me do it, made me sequester myself there, down in the dirt-clod kingdom of bent nails and wire cuttings, listening to the men talk about their women and their cars, their sports bets, their nights out drinking or barbeques at home? I had yet to read the famous Poe story, but I could hear, I thought, below the scraping of their trowels and the rough friction of brick against brick, the beating of my own heart. The dank, dimming underworld of the house smelled of wet mortar and cut wood, of earth and gasoline. So, this was how one made one's way among men? What more would be expected of me? Who would I become? Above us, far above all the busied hands and the browned backs, the rusty trucks and dumpsters, the sun shone as it had for millions—billions—of years. And of all those days, it was this one that placed me there.

I don't know why I pretended to be walled in alive. It is, in fact, pretty much my worst adult nightmare. Maybe it excited me to approach fear without needing to feel it fully. I suspect I felt as much about manhood. The men, too, may have sensed that I needed to be close to them, close enough to glimpse their world, yet remain safe at its threshold. What I remember still are their disembodied voices, deep-throated, raspy, of different tenors, sometimes laughing, sometimes derisive, sometimes utterly sincere. I think now it was less a burial and more a type of cocoon enwrapping me in those tones. The call and response of ongoing inside jokes. The frustrated rants about what wasn't getting done. The shrill mockery of some; the near reverence of others. The prodding and cajoling; the shunning and the sharing—this was all part of the transformation of my own throat, the first stage of the change from which I would emerge and be heard.

Cathedral

It is mid-July and the A/C is broken. The front door is propped wide open and even from the street, with its few passing cars and tractors, you can hear the harsh sounds of billiard balls meeting and dispersing on the one table inside. It is dark and hazy—a gray-blue smoke that swirls in simple patterns against light from the few filmy windows. In the time it has taken him to lean his bike against the blazing white side of the building and make his way to the bartender, the entire world has altered. He sees things now as his father sees them, through a filter of cheap bourbon and regret. The floor and bar are sticky. Everything about the place seems burdened.

The boy is here from the farm with a message from his mother. She knows better than to have her husband called to the phone. The message is short and neutral in tone. She has learned to keep her expectations small. Supper will be on the table at five o'clock.

The boy can leave now, but instead he steps back unnoticed into the stacks of longneck boxes. There is something about this place. There is something about the men hunkered separately, yet together, over their drinks, talking in secret tones, the boy almost understands. It is like a church, the boy thinks, but it is a different stained glass that casts this light and it is the bartender who presides over it all as if offering up communion. Which he is, of sorts, though the boy won't fully comprehend for decades to come.

Long years later, in AA meetings, the boy will recount that moment in the cathedral. He will recall his father, head bowed, talking among men, shoulder to shoulder at the bar with empty shot glasses upended near their beer bottles. He will recall how even before he stole that first beer and shoved it deep into his pocket, even before he drank it in the barn and felt that first gentle dulling he would come to need, it was as if the room spoke to him. And the smoke said *our time here is brief.* And the light said *we only look when we are made to see.* And the holy spirits said *no one will ever love you like we do.*

Uncle Frank

The children are in their sixties now. They are rarely shirtless, except when they shower. Unless you count gardening, they don't play in the dirt. And yet I recognize each in this photo easily, these adults-to-be, squatting here by the old well pump, muddy and beaming. The faces have sharpened, come into a kind of focus, but the features have always been the same, year upon year. They are perhaps four to six years old, these three cousins. It is a hot day and my uncle is sweat-soaked, watching over them. He is supposed to be teaching them something about the farm, but he is just thinking he needs a beer and a smoke, and he can't leave and he can't take the kids with him to the VFW. The women are shopping in town and Nellie has the truck, anyway. He thought he had an extra pack of Chesterfields in his dresser, but did not. He wants to work on the tractor, but the kids won't leave him be. They are like the barn cats at milking time, all under his feet, always needing something. He doesn't know how the ladies do it. He can't even stay near the transistor radio like he wants. They flit all over the yard. They are always finding something they want him to look at or explain or hem and haw about— some critter or bauble, no matter how minor.

It might be different if one of these belonged to him. Being a dad might change something, he guesses. But he doesn't feel any wish like that in himself. There isn't any tug at his heart. In fact, he worries now. In fact, he's been thinking about it ever since the women left—what if she starts wanting what her sisters have, what if she wants a baby after all and right away? He'll say no and what then? When is the last time she really took that for an answer? All he knows is the VFW would be cool and dim and smoky and the Falstaff would be icy against his palms and it would freeze his throat a little drinking the first half in one gulp. He's mad that he's here. It is not a man's place, after all, to herd the kids.

This is when he decides it. Right there. He thinks: if these young'uns need to know about life on the farm, I can show them something. He gets down his Remington .22 from the rack and calls the cousins to come with him. He's taking them to the barn. They will get their lesson. They can watch him see to that sick momma barn cat.

Well, you can imagine. It turns the whole day on its head. When the ladies get home, the kids are still crying over it, hunkered in the house. My mom says what happened and my sister, choking back tears, sobs, says, Uncle Frank shot a pigeon and fed it to the cat. Everybody turns to Frank for an explanation, but he's in the truck already on his way down the dusty driveway and out toward town. He'll have to answer for it, eventually, but for the moment, the radio is tuned just the way he likes it and he's found half a pack of cigs in his glove box. Things are looking up.

Devil's Food Cake

She likes to make the cakes herself. She gets all her ideas from magazines, she confesses that, but she doesn't buy pre-shaped molds. She bakes sheet cakes and sculpts them just the way she wants—maybe a turtle, say, maybe a giraffe—once, she even made a kangaroo. The kids, she thinks, feel more special that way. Last year, her youngest was in tears when the time came to eat his dinosaur.

She likes everything about it. The flour sifting softly into the bowl, the sugar you can hardly tell that from, and the deep gold of the egg yolk breaking into and over all the glistening oil. Then the way the beaters blend it all together and smooth it out. You can't do that with the rest of your life. Real life, everyday living, is lumpy and never quite gets the ingredients right. One phone call from an old boyfriend and the world gets tilted on its axis. One missing spark plug wire and you can't drive anywhere.

The magazines, though, are good company. Women in their pages are always going someplace fancy and planning something neat. Their hair is perfect and their kids get 'A's in school. Well, at least her kids do like school. They'd rather be there than at home, she suspects, the way things are at supper, sometimes. Tom can be hard to predict. You just never knew. He could be sweet as turtle pie or he could blow a fuse over the teensiest thing. He likes having things a certain way. He just isn't always certain about which way that is. Take, for instance, yesterday—while she was making angel food, which is harder to time right, he came home early and wanted his supper on the table by four o'clock. Well, you just can't have two things in the oven at once. And it was Michael's birthday, what was she supposed to do? She said she'd sooner take a beating than throw that cake away. Sounded confident about it, too. Which is what, she guesses, tipped her hand, and why she's forbidden to use her own car, sitting by the phone, thumbing through ladies' magazines. . . .

Water, cake flour, sugar, butter, baking soda, eggs, vanilla extract, sometimes a cup of cocoa powder. A pinch of this; a dash of that. There would always be a new recipe that worked better than what she had. You just needed to keep tasting.

Beauty, 1976

We're crammed around the fold-down kitchenette table
B.J. couldn't find the leaf for. I have to hook one arm around
Tommy just to lift my coffee. "Camille," B.J. says, "it's been
a long night, we're kinda hungry, you can hustle it up?"
Their newest baby's in its car seat in the sink—the near
window is blurred as a moldy shower curtain, still, a weak
sun is dawning on her and I can almost make out an
antenna on the neighbor's trailer. Three pickups and a
Pinto have left for work, so far. I'd know a Pinto's tail-
lights anywhere—I'm pretty sure their gas tanks used to
explode. Pinned to one wall, the July Harley calendar has
hollow red hearts inked into every Saturday, blanched
Christmas cards taped at each corner—ice skaters, angels,
snow-covered sleds. I'm almost sober, but my fork shakes
so much, the eggs keep slipping off. I'd like to trap them
with my toast, but how with one hand? "Beej," Billy sighs,
passing his flask, "this is sure something—don't let her
get away from you."

The Hitching Post

You are not sure what compels you, but just for kicks you sit on the coin-operated motorcycle at the entrance to Kmart. You don't have quarters, but you ride it anyway, all the way back to 1964, when it was a covered wagon outside The Hitching Post Bar and Grill. That place burned down and the lot was never built on again, though there was nothing sacred buried there but the remains of several marriages. You are in the wagon's seat with a set of chapped leather reins in your hand. The reins are stapled to the tongue of the wagon, though—there are no traces, let alone horses. But that doesn't matter, it is a real Conestoga one, just like in the westerns that dominate the TV listings and you are going somewhere, headed yonder, away from the strictures of enforced bedtimes and tooth brushings and toward adventure in a land far vaster and more promising than Peoria, Illinois. Behind you, the wagon body is stuffed with trash from the parking lot—pint bottles, beer cans, newspapers. This is also where they keep the rake and hedge trimmers, and if you were older you might recognize that at least one drunk couple has lain together there, but you are only eight and thinking about the towering mesas, the fellowship of ranch hands in their bunkhouses, and the vulture swallows soaring in ever narrowing circles above the parking lot. You are thinking that this gold has got to get through to the bank in Denver. This shipment, used condoms or no, means life or death to the little town of Dry Gulch, whose citizens work so hard to maintain civilization in the wilderness. They have a modest church and schoolhouse; they have a general store. Moms and dads pitch in there to ensure their kids' safety and manners and work ethics. They don't hit them for forgetting to feed the dog; they don't sneak off to saloons with each other's spouses.

When you finally dismount the motorcycle, you can't remember what you came for. Maybe it was just engine oil, but wasn't there something else? You had meant for this gesture to be whimsical and spontaneous, something you haven't been in years, but it has ridden off with you now, the wagon ruts extending deeply into the past. Your wife is calling, embarrassed, but there is no returning to the present as the same boy. Within two years, your parents will divorce. And that austere wagon, it will be loaded with everything you own, headed irrevocably westward, and very much alone, into your stoic, stolid, stultifying life.

News and Tobacco

In 1963, the magazine racks were still largely black and white and there was a grainy light around the parked cars when you stepped out onto the sidewalk your whole town depended on. One pack of candy cigarettes could last two days in a boy's t-shirt pocket, their ends whittled to soggy pencil points, the other still intact with its amorphous dot of red dye #2, kept lit by the glare off windshields and the glance of a homecoming queen from her throne of crepe flowers. Never mind the gum wad stuck between the sole of your sneaker and the pedal of your bike, never mind the rivets of your jeans hot enough to brand your palms; if you could find him, your pop would spring for a bottle of Coke just to shoo you from the dim VFW and the stool reserved eventually for you.

But not for a while yet, not until you outgrew the banana seat and butterfly handlebars and the washed-out stumps twisted along the river banks; not until you had been beaten into cruelty or submission by the older boys who were always there before you, no matter where you went, ready to dunk you in the municipal pool or punch your arm to prove they had fists at the ends of theirs. All you wanted was a little quiet to dream in, a basement with no drama venting from above: no sad, sappy soap opera eternally on; no sister with her heart broken, eternally on; no parents bickering over budgets, eternally on....

It's all so much a shadow box now, a dollhouse with an open back, each memory in its compartment, the furniture in miniature, the people still and suspended like fruit cocktail in pale gelatin. The silence you wanted has become so loud with loss, that angle-parked this morning beside E-Vapor Smoke Shop, you hesitate and recall your father's arm around you to work the column shift, the little plastic Jesus, his arms uplifted on the dash; you see how you've always had control of some steering and nothing else. You don't say when you stop and start; you don't say how fast or slow. And in truth, fate has often determined which way to go.

So, no wonder you are confused now, divorced, faced with a sudden multitude of choices. Times change, unlike your father, who never could. That's your heart you can hear in the motor's idling, eternally on, eternally travelling, even when you're sitting still. Maybe you don't have to be back at work. Maybe you don't need to be home by five. Maybe you don't want to be here at all.

You Are Now Free to Move about the Cabin

The little girl across the aisle positions a souvenir sea shell over her baby brother's nose, explaining he's just dialed 911, the smoke is everywhere and he has five minutes to live, but it's ok, he paid attention when mommy was talking to him, he has procedure. I'm not sure whether he's supposed to breathe from it or speak into it, but what our future flight attendant understands is that you have to take action with what's at hand: you adjust your seat back once a minute, you pretend to vomit in the airsickness bag; you divide the pretzels from your remaining Chex Mix and conquer. But the boy, he totes his one world everywhere, he has no use for anything even vaguely unfamiliar and insists on his inalienable right to unearth the idyllic barnyard scene stamped in the one trusty bowl he'll snack from. Let the plane plummet spiraling into the Western Plains, he'll still be in Topeka with his favorite blanket and cows. Indeed, down down down there, the white frame farmhouses seem no more than juice boxes cornered on tidy breakfast trays. The huge mounds of hay bunkered in huger black tarps seem like raisins in bran. And now down down down through the clouds of Cremora in coffee, percolated on the stove, though mother had given her an electric one, I can see my grandmother wringing a hand towel as some stranger packs her stemware. Her hand trembles, her pallid cheeks twitch. I am shocked to see that kitchen so clearly, after forty-five years, to know the floor plan of that small-town tract home, where the sink was, for instance, below the one kitchen window she gazed from as she washed—a hummingbird feeder, just outside, not an ounce of nectar in it. And now she is slapping at one of the movers, weakly, with a dishtowel, lashing out as if he were a thief, as if he were taking everything she owned, which of course he is, and as if she would never see it all again, which of course she truly won't. While I, I am playing drums on the half-opened, half-filled moving boxes or reading the funny papers instead of wrapping plates. It's easy enough to see how children become nuisances, just being themselves. There comes a day when playtime is over, when you don't have the strength to dissolve a sugar cube in water. The birds move on, your children stop paying the rent and the next thing you know is a nursing home room the width of a closet. Speaking of which, take good care of her piano. And don't you dare lose those mittens she knitted for Christmas. Grandma's little helper must survive to grow old.

The Storm-Torn Edge of Heaven

The wind lifts some of the bed sheets sideways and others billow almost straight up. The old woman must tug the lines down to clip the pins on. She can't be seen, tending to the linens, but without her there would be no sky at all, no dusk or dawn of variance, no tumultuous layering of cloud and color. Even when the sky seems clear, which is to say, when there is only one cloud over all things, just very high, she is there at each corner, without fail, making certain no edge of heaven so much as grazes the ground.

There was a time I believed this story, even as I made it up. There were times when storms blackened the sky and I knew her ire as I knew my own, that she would have to pull down the entire sky and start over, that she would knead and knead until the covers wrung white again, crisp as the starched edge of an old man's Sunday shirt collar, a sky that seemed less to pass over than to hover protectively far beyond my own reach and powers. Just when did the actual subsume the imagined? When did grade school science supplant the realms of gossamer and glitter, those fiercely held first beliefs let go of, at last?

It just happens. One day you look at the clouds and see clouds; mere canopies or scrims of moisture beneath which the whole of earth turns. And you never think again of the old woman's stout legs and weary, arthritic fingers, the unwavering patience and devotion of her work, her just and gentle oversight—all those projections of a grace you once knew, that is now lost, as distant as the sky itself— of which you rarely think, at which you rarely look, but which stretches forth beyond you, whether noticed or not.

Chutes and Ladders

When I say the season was fading, imagine August sent through the wash cycle an umpteenth time; it was truly more of a dim, golden blush, as if the evening was embarrassed at just how deeply it felt for us. Silly to think, I know, but I'd say 3,000 cubic feet of that light to the pound—it had some weight to it, it made me feel held and firmly in place, smelling of late summer as it did—new cut grasses, hot asphalt, honeysuckle—and circulating as if forced through a fan, inching forward one throw of the dice at a time—a leisurely evening board game, the strategies of which were to move when you were told, follow the directions on the cards life had in store, do not stop, skip the sad parts, by all means pass go.

Like childhood, it was simple and yet deeply connected to some knowledge just out of reach, something *in place*, and yet out of it, like one game's pieces used in another— Monopoly's silver race car or Clue's candlestick, but traversing the board of Candy Land or Sorry—stories within stories plotted square by square, whether to that blind roll of mismatched dice or a bent arrow spun on its pie wheel of colors—our journeys funneled through inherited passages, fortunes good or ill—and to be familial, to be *familiar*, was to exist only in relation to that whole— the torn box that held it all, taped and re-taped, with its tattered food-stained rules and decades of used scorecards—all vouchsafed for keeping, to the youngest, always, since being the last to die, we were allowed to win.

History

Jack, there is so much I no longer need to know, yet can't
forget. Directions to houses I'll never visit again, knots
I'll never tie, the petty faults of people who have long
since died. Were I not referring to them now, I would not
have need to, ever. The moment for many dates and names
has passed. Though Francois' obsession with prostate
function, your own issues with hair in the tub, are not
quite history, I suppose. History being lessons in
interrelations of some scale—events and developments
that reverberate through cultures. No, the world turns
quite well without a poem about bathroom etiquette or
Ida Knudson's Persian cat. But then it is not the coursings
of history that bring "Lisa" to mind in me. Not the West's
clash with Middle-Eastern politics, nor décor's debt to
Iranian rugs, no, I am thinking about Midnight and
Mischief, Brownie and Muffin and Reginald and King.
Rulers? Patriots? Agents of change? No, just sages of
patience and kindness and responsibility. Those exemplars
of unconditional love, of submission to necessity, of
courage and ferocity in the face of the unknown. Velcro,
Duchess, Kiki, Sarge. Susan's Shadow. That little wiener
dog, Napoleon, three houses down. A luxury, some would
say, to spend one's morning with the names of past pets—
a legislator's prime argument against tenure, if there ever
was one—but I remember Sufi in your lap as you were
dying, what it meant to you to feel that steady heart. And
Ida's emaciated hand smoothing the fur of her old tomcat,
who prowled all night, but by day deigned to lie coddled
and spoken to, though utterly misnamed, when there was
no one else for Ida, no one left at all.

The Present

is this chilled pear we share in the dark, knowing that
were our dog Beau still here, he would wake near the bed,
steadfast and stoic, until you passed down the core. We
will hear him licking there, for decades, absorbed…that
taste forgotten, then recalled, in the grain of the floor.

Knossos

I can still see us there, laughing, all five photographing each other photographing each other, our faces masked by the cameras aimed at one another, and there in the far background, the ruins of ancient Greece. Crete, to be specific, Knossos, to be more so, though not much Minoan civilization even enters the frame. It is all about the present, just twenty-one years old, set loose in the world for a semester abroad, these ruins doubly lost on us, unaware there'd come a time we would forget each other's names. No, we didn't get it then, the innumerable feet that had worn these stone paths, whether the ancients themselves or centuries of tourists, those individual pasts each as unique and vibrant as ours, all gone, vanished into the labyrinth of history, utterly erased. Yet they had their names, they experienced achievements and failures, they had their children, they put to use their allotted time. And in memory, perhaps because I am closer now to the border between worlds, I think I can sense the multitudes, the ghost throngs that had gone before us, how they shuffled the paths between us, how they lay down beside us on the ferry, a humanity that fed us, urged us forward, day by day. This is the end ordained in our beginning, the bestial clarity and solace we ignore as we seek: we would be nothing without them, we will be nothing with them and we must learn to look upon this without turning away.

II. Readiness

Here

What he remembers most viscerally about that night is swimming naked in the small county lake, but feeling tips of tree branches against his abdomen and genitals—the stark panic at first, before he realized what it was, then an unsettling sense that he was swimming in the sky— a kind of cloud of flesh, weightless, adrift in the dark. The lake had been formed when a new dam was built, flooding old growth forest, and huge oaks still stood upright beneath the water, some reaching so near the surface, that in dryer seasons, their furthermost branches revealed themselves, as if the withered fingers of entreating hands. Treading water, he had the sensation of drowning within his body, the night sky oceanic, its scattered stars surrounding him, up and down seeming not so much reversed as irrelevant and impossible to determine; so odd to be so small and yet so sensitive to space, to tremble in the tensing chill of fluid and damp air. He recalls turning on his back to assure himself, his breath deep and rapid, knowing in his heart he was just yards from shore, but understanding, finally, how little that shore meant in the immensity of experience. It was nothing, in fact, it could not be trusted, there was only, against the terror of this freedom, his own will, his own perspective—he could fear it or not, he could drink from it or drown in it—and though he did not yet know what to do and how to live his life, he knew the choice now, knew it *was* a choice, no matter how inconsequential in the vast realms of history, the consequences were his: he would be lost; he would be found; he would learn this over and over again; he would be many things, but never, ever, anyplace but here.

Focus

There are so many choices, so many instances and accidents of being, and no way to foresee which is the essential one, the one that will later cast all others into context. For a moment, say, you remove your glasses, a bleary, sweeping glance, the verdant lawn darkening beneath dusk's weight, the fireflies beginning their starry, dew-gemmed mating, sky and earth reversed now, the trees' roots threading what once was air. For a moment, you look aside and the present is gone, just vanished, a kind of illusion staged with mirrors and misdirection, and there is instead a mere handful of lit windows, each so far from others as to be virtually alone, and try as you might, no degree of will brings them closer together.

There is, in fact, an ever-increasing distance to be bridged, an ever-blurring expanse and the songs of the lost—newly hatched and sprung from early summer's soil, the incessant, insistent tones of dumb, stubborn desire— traverse the restless, oceanic lawn, its fireflies now like a few sparsely scattered ships, bound to ancient coordinates of presence and absence, alone with what progress the winds and tides allow. As you are, you understand, stripped of pretense and arrogance and the lit rooms of your illusions, overtaken by the sheer enormity, made insular and solitary, given a threshold you can approach but not cross, the patterns of light becoming now more alien, harder to decipher, no longer patterns at all, just appearances, energies, however briefly and tentatively, making themselves known.

Readiness

In the dream, I am ironing. This is a notable change of pace. No one has chased me anywhere; there is no complex circuitry to decode before some tragic detonation. I am just pressing shirts and blouses, one sleeve at a time, draping one half over the discolored board while I steam collars and seams. I am doing it the only way I know how, the way my mother did, patiently, without speaking, rarely glancing toward the TV she listened to. Somewhere, I read a man can't really say he knows fatherhood until he's washed and folded his children's clothes; I would add to that, bagging things for Goodwill. Those narrow waists, the slender neck openings, the faint stains I couldn't quite remove, always proof of all they had outgrown. But in my dream, there is none of that poignant nostalgia, there is just the ironing, precisely carried out, piece after piece. There is no deep meaning to be mined. I am not preparing for some gala event. I am not re-envisioning my life. I am just steaming and pressing, the rustle of fabric pronounced in the silent room, the hiss of the iron loud against that silence, my arm moving forward and back, my other hand resetting the shirt against the board's cushioned edge. If I wished, the iron could have shrunk smaller and smaller in my hand. Or it could have been attached to my wrist like a fist. I could have used two irons in concert like cymbals or defibrillator paddles. But in the dream, there was nothing disjunctive or strange, the shirts just hung along a curtain rod, the fronts perfectly buttoned, their arms relaxed at their sides. There was no *like* and no *as if*, there was no *before* or *after which*. And yet this dream resonates in me like few others. The shirts hung in the shapes of persons. Those shapes hung collectively in the colors and postures of a family. Whose is not important, the dream insists. There is no such thing as emptiness. There is only being ready.

Four Coasts

Just now, I have been reading a poem by Morton Marcus, who is dead, as he writes about reading the poems of George Seferis, who was then, and is still, dead also. I write this in hope that, in its reading, you will understand something of the gift I have been given, here, in winter, the space heater, like the nightlights of my childhood, aglow on my lower legs, even these swollen ankles not aching for once—that here in the comfort, and something near to peace, of this very early North Carolina morning, I am alive to carry their names forward, in some small way; to say I am here, because they were here, before me. All along the Atlantic coast, there are immense warehouses, stacks of cargo containers in freight depots, filled with unopened boxes of priceless goods— sidetracked, mismarked, forgotten and idle. One pays one's homage. Either you keep going or you don't. Seferis, Marcus says, became history himself, walking the ruins of the ancients. Though, I have met George, also, and I know there were many kisses between wars. As for Morton, I met his widow in Santa Cruz, to whom I vowed to teach her husband's poems for as long as I was able. This, I think, is all poets do. We try to keep our promises, to be here when you turn the page and open the hold. And it does not matter, reader, if none of the three of us is alive now; if I have vanished or will always be just a few states away, writing before dawn, my old legs elevated, a journal in my lap. It is the moment worth naming, I hope to have left you. The one that made me cock my head and hear Greek fishermen in the fog, laughing, cursing the exasperating, slow journey home to their women, especially being just off California, as they are, which anyone can tell, even as far away as here.

The Page

I am blessed to have this art, this ritual, mornings, which begins each day centering what is most myself. The only constant, year by year, making sense when little else does; I am here, it tells me—another day and you are still here. It has never been, as I once thought, about having something to say. It has always been the listening, the recognition of something hinted at, but as yet unheard; some clue as to the shifting ontological coordinates at which I exist. The decades have accrued. The women in my life, bless each and every one, those women have come and gone, but the paper remains here in front of me, constant; my true wife, I fear. I have become, ultimately, who I was authored to be. That night in Greece, say, when it was stormy on Aegina, and I was hunkered in a hotel not far from the sea, warmed by cigarettes and retsina, writing by one candle that flickered wildly. I did not know just who I would become, but I knew what I would have to do, that words would be at the heart of it, poems and more poems, then, finally, books. Earlier in the evening, I heard the fishermen slapping octopi dead against the docks, the gulls shrill and expectant overhead; saw the sunlight dissolve in the coppery green harbor, the late trawlers make their way into port. And I was overlooking it all, in my spartan room, sporadic ocean drafts foretelling the storm to come, I was above it so fully I might as well have been orchestrating it—it felt that right, that attuned to who I was. In truth, I knew right where this was leading, I knew thirty-seven years ago, that this separateness was never going to pass, no matter who I slept with: I would always wake up alone, insular, struggling with my own boundaries; I would always be far from any home, adrift, at the edges of water and earth; but should the storm swell or subside, I would be safe within it, hunkered over my pages, casting my net of words, as I am now, in the only way I know how.

Nightlight

It was just a nightlight beside my bed, a four-watt bulb in a plain electrical outlet, yet it transformed, late nights, into something ethereal and strange. Sometimes insects were drawn to it, and as their shadows elongated, swelled and shifted, the beige wall flickered with primitive beings, as if I were in some ancient cave while a shaman chalked a bear hunt with a charred stick. Around me were the damp sounds of my brother's rhythmic breathing, the hollow rasp of the electric clock's second hand, rubbing as it crossed the minute and the hour, and outside there might be wind in the eaves, not howling exactly, but something akin to soft moans of surprise and awareness. There was something surreal in the experience and there on that scuffed wall, in that miniature dusk stenciled with act and accident, a sense of foreboding was born in me, a sense of wonder. There evolved a measure of pageantry and grandeur I had not experienced, the sense that my life had direction I alone did not control. There would be light to which I would be drawn, there would be shadows in which I would always live, shadows too big for the bodies that cast them. It would be something sacred and primal, played out behind gauze curtains, a solitary inward journey of story and song.

Patrimony

Even at ten, the boy knows that destiny will not call for everyone, that there is only so much memory in the world, someone must be forgotten. When smoke materializes from the stove vent to meet the wind—just before it straightens its tie, as if about to knock, as if about to pitch a deal—it's just making room for what comes next. This moment is not, they said, the boy's business. He is supposed to play pretend in the yard, while the adults have coffee in the kitchen. He is not supposed to hear their tense voices through the fogged glass and he knows he should find yet another stick and gouge yet another hole in the earth, that beneath the crabgrass there is a further story seething with insects he once forced into jars. But he is a writer, this boy, and the voices collect in him, he wants to be a writer, so he jabs air holes into his head, he chews some grass, he lets dew collect on his teeth, because the voices have to live, the voices have to huddle, afraid, in their own shit, before dying in him. That way, he knows he alone can smell the coffee sixty years after, only he can hear his mother weeping and the neighbors turning to each other, gossiping behind hands, as if that weak gesture could keep the wind from their words. It is sunset, the sky seems scarred, but it is only the momentary wounds of clouds, the wind is changeless. Who has done what and for what reason, he was never to know, but he could feel it when car tires crushed the sticks he threw in the street, he could feel himself coming apart and being carried away. And now, even today there are scuffs on the wind's dress shoes, dust from the stoop of that tenement the grown boy leaned against, knocking his pipe empty, before brushing shoulders with ten thousand other nameless men, few of whom noticed your grandfather making his way to your life.

Hard Labor

You can say that it is about the breath we all share, the test of life we all face, that it is about empathy and the loving observation of those with whom we inhabit this earth, but, please, let us admit, at root, it is about one's own loneliness. We writers, we are in exile from a country far inside ourselves, that we cannot return to, ever, and we are making our way in a new world, among strangers we must come to care about for the first time. Pavese was bone lonely there, watching others live their lives; this was his labor, that he was not living fully and in the same way. We know this, at bottom, about ourselves. Though we fight it dutifully with our initiatives and our outreach. It is our solitary natures that drive programs into the schools and communities. But then it has ever been so. You can speak of noble aspirations, you can speak of a literature that binds a people together, but really, you are just a slave to your distances, your solitude being a deeper wound. You walk the streets, those about you intent on their futures. You alone seem to be watching it all happen. People look only where they walk, consult their phones, inhabit their reflections in subway windows, always between places. There is, in this life with others, always the sense of unfinished business. They pass each other on the sidewalk without so much as brushing clothes, making their way home to secret lives of romance or subterfuge or desperation or evil. You never really know. But for today it is enough to have noticed the woman in the tan suit and olive blouse with breasts so much like a girl you loved once, now dead of cancer. It is enough to have seen her make her way from one street corner to the next, swaying in the way that women do and to have felt for a moment an old hunger, gentled by time, but fully present and to have remembered loving and being loved, if only for the instant it took for her to dissolve into the multitude around you.

Night Sky above Bassae

That sky is a kind of book with black pages. Then stars appear, cluster by cluster, syllables first, then whole sentences, shivering faintly in the frost of their fire. A passage it has taken thirty-five years to translate—still on my back, still clasping the thin wool blanket to my throat, the Greek ruins I lie within, unguarded, fenceless, bordered only by their own felled walls. To sleep on stone is to enter it. To be stilled by history is to age. What you are becomes who you are. Carbons, calcium, water, salt— basic compounds, simple chains loosing into... what? Desire? Design?

When the bus returns, as one does each morning, to complete its mountain route up or down, as may be the case—when that bus stops, the young man I was will step up into it and its patrons, feel his clothing rubbed against others', the smell of simple breakfasts and tobacco and Turkish coffee on their breaths. He will hear the chickens squawking from their woven cages. And I will have reentered the story of the living, once again a paying passenger, jolted along, vaguely claustrophobic, but now a poet, more or less.

Wrought

Jack, our old age together lasted twenty minutes. The distillation of all we'd learned about economy. While well-tanned college boys walked their dogs and loaded surfboards into vans, we sat rocking on the rented beach house porch—something we had joked about for years, the inevitable old poets' home—and listened to gulls scavenge along the water.

There was a weathered resin owl mounted a few feet above your head, meant I am sure, to deter birds from roosting under the eaves, from crapping up just this sort of picturesque moment. Just why we associate owls with wisdom—as opposed to violent death—I am not sure. They can see in the dark? They oversee the woods? Their heads rotate so flexibly that they can see their past as well as their future? But in retrospect, it makes me think of the calm you had attained. You were who you were. Not without struggle, of course. Over the years, you waged a war in yourself. But by the last, when finality was amassing just offshore, you had come to terms.

Overwrought: is that phrase rooted in reference to writing or making? Wrought as in wrought iron, I suppose. Shaped material, patterns worked by designers and artisans, grief. When the fashion of many was over-making, a flair for the dramatic or reflexive digression, you set off on a quest for simplicity. You kept paring away. Divesting yourself of the extraneous long before the trials of chemotherapy and transplant lists.

Who carved the first apple out of stone and what artist ate of it? The false hope and desire to live on in our work. Such work lives, but it is a life unto its own, our reality less important as the work travels on. In the end, the work is happy to be shed of us, to stand without biography and bias, to step into its place, reader by reader. Or maybe, in the end the work circles around and back to roost right where it started, inextricable from the decisions we made, aesthetics we pledged our lives to. Perhaps artists can't be distinguished from the history they convey and in conveying, make. Or if they are separated, it is by a pane like glass that reflects the inner world even as the outer is seen through it. That storm door, let's say, you paused at a long while before closing behind you. The one that shimmers a bit and rattles when the winds pass, but whose latch holds its own.

Apples

Who is to say which moments your kids will look back on, which photograph will be etched in air for the whole of their lives, a touchstone they'll return to when thinking of you or a particular tenor of day or light. Perhaps it is the one where he is set apart from you, in the embrace of a bear statue, overwhelmed by shadow and magnitude, feeling small; or the one in which he is dressed up as a superhero but is crying for help; or perhaps it is when she holds baby brother, no one knowing she'd grow up to be childless and bereft. The uncle who died of cancer is always still smoking. The family friend who died in the wreck is still waving from behind the wheel. And here, their dead father, forever forty-six and poised to blow out the candles on a cake shaped like Illinois. Who knew? Who suspected that this card table, folded even now in a niche by the furnace, would signify an era of birthdays? Who could have predicted how important this would all be, that the clouds would be amassed in just this pattern, just this once, ever, in a billion years, and their reflection mirrored on the water would seem a double negative of sorts, pooling, about to run over the spillway and into the turbines of the teeming present? The sherbet never melts in its single serving bowls. The sky never dissipates into any other time of day. Your mother and father, bless them, had long enough lives to make peace with death. They could look back and see how richly they had lived. They finally felt it was selfish to want any more. That's not something you explain. What you know, is that you must sort these carefully, making certain each child gets his or her portion of history. It is important that things be equal. It is important that even now, so far away, they not forget. These photos, say, of the stray burro, with its head poked in the car window, begging apple slices, stopping traffic right in the middle of the road. You remember how much the kids loved its nuzzling at their palms. You used to think of it often, mornings, when you had someone to core those apples for.

Kodak Moment, 1987

Each child has a camera, the youngest, a disposable, and each holds it to their face, completely blocking the real view of where they are, the present in which they stand. They are 6, 9 and 13, respectively, aligned by age along the fence of a petting zoo where the eager goats and lone pony have come, assuming they'll be fed. This is a moment apart. Just as the children set it to one side, the father, too, has snapped this photograph, also capturing his wife's hand with a brown paper bag, just inside the frame, coming to her children, bringing them the cracked corn soon to be nuzzled from their palms. Wherefrom this impulse? To anticipate and capture experience before living it? To collect experience while separate from its process, pinning it to memory like a brittle butterfly to foam-board? Is it or is it not a shame that a picture of the pony seems to mean more than the pony itself?

The father is seventy years old now, long divorced and those children long grown. As far as he knows, this is the one photo that survived. It has lain layered in the strata of family snapshots for over thirty years. If only he could remember taking it! Perhaps the children were drained and cranky after an arduous day of vacation driving. Perhaps he and his wife felt intimate, conspiring to bring them joy. Perhaps his little daughter adored the pony and asked to take it home. It's true, there is his shadow in every photo he's ever taken, but there is nothing to relive now but the implicit gesture of photography itself. Having stood there apart, distanced, watching.

Suncatchers

His sister is home already. A school bus drops her off at the door to their apartment building. The boy, though, has a short walk home, first along 57th Street, then west on McNeill. There is a row of fast food franchises on the latter, so he usually grabs takeout before the dinner rush. Their father works even later now. He will check on them by phone around 4:30, just to make sure they are safely there. After that, who knows when he'll get in. Sometimes the two are in bed already, having left schoolwork to sign on the breakfast nook table. The boy looks up into the glass and steel that rises around him on all sides. It seems he lives in a world of mirrors, mirrors that reflect only other mirrors. From the street, the windows, with the sun striking them, seem the blazing scales of some book's ancient beast. He walks faster, but not out of fear. He doesn't want his sister's shake to melt. He's almost there. Mike the doorman spots him at the corner, toots his whistle and waves him into the crosswalk.

Upstairs, the girl has set up TV trays in front of the sofa. She has lost weight since March. He brings her bigger portions, but that doesn't seem to matter. She stands at the apartment's picture window and looks across into the office building across the way. The business of the world is getting finished. Papers are being stacked, desk drawers are being opened and closed, files are being filed, phones are being answered. None of it seems real to her. Everything now seems temporary. When her brother arrives, they will choose a movie. It will be hard to watch, it always is, but they can't help doing it. At the park feeding ducks, a Christmas morning, a day at the zoo. Somehow, it doesn't matter that they've seen them before; there is something new to focus on every time. They ask each other questions. They help each other remember. In some, her brother is so young that she is nowhere to be found. Time, now *that* is real. Sometimes they pause or slow the movie, so it doesn't pass as quickly. You can truly see the faces then, the small changes in features between smiles and complete sentences. Sometimes her brother goes to the screen and points things out in the background, things he remembers that she does not. Sometimes they freeze Mother's face right as she is talking to them. And they finish homework that way, while her suncatchers in the window flare brightly, then dim.

Home

He's not sure what to do about the mice. To move the nest outside will mean death to these babies, a prolonged death without their mother, who has retreated into the recesses of the house. He could leave them in the drawer, but that seems uncivilized and unacceptable, now that he has seen them. He has to do something. They are feeble, enmeshed together, wriggling to maintain their warm, individual places. They have not yet opened their eyes on this world, but they are still distressed by the sudden light.

He has opened the drawer to get some nice linen napkins that once belonged to his mother. He was going to use them for a dinner date he is planning. Most are ruined. If they haven't been chewed into shreds for bedding, they have been urinated and shat upon. It was a drawer that never got opened in a bureau that was rarely used. The mice had been undisturbed for generations. They had history there. They thought themselves safe.

Just a few weeks ago, he took his youngest son to college. He remembers returning home alone. How hollow the house seemed to him, yet how much activity it had known. He knew he would eventually have to leave it, but would not know how. Could the mice feel anything like this about the bureau? He would have to poison the adults. There was no way to trap and release them all. But there is the very real dilemma of what to do with these babies. He could just leave them in the yard and let nature take its course. They would be eaten or die slowly of exposure. Or he could drown them—hold them all underwater in a bucket, one by one. This death would be less violent than blows from a shovel, but less immediate. They would struggle frantically to live.

In the end, he closes the drawer and leaves the room without what he came for. He leaves them untouched for now. Let them grow up and die like the rest of us, he thinks. The damage is already done. In a few months, he will start spreading poison; he will take his home back and perhaps even get it ready for sale. He will protect what is his. But they will have had their time to run in its walls, to appreciate it, too. They will have opened their eyes and found their lives happening, if only for a while.

Suicide

He's not sure just why he did it now, now that he is outside his body, beyond the straight razor and all the blood. There is so much of that. He had not imagined so much could be held in his one container—that flesh, which only moments ago had felt so small and insignificant.

To be truthful, he is surprised he had the courage to see it through. The first slice was tentative, with a long moment to catch his breath before plunging on. Ironic, yes, and yes, in the end, not even he knows why. He had his whole life ahead of him, you will say, but he foresaw no relief. He was beaten, surely. His friends died or disappeared. His infrequent meds failed. He just tired of the struggle it takes to stay alive. He foresaw only narrow years of poverty and addiction, blown like litter on these streets, without purpose, and with no connection to most people any longer, a mere shadow amongst flesh and blood. How many days seeped out into night at the edges of this city?

How many times had he told himself he could go home, if he wanted. But home was like a poster now in one of those travel agency windows; it was a distant, unreachable place existing only in the mind. There was no bus that could take you there. It was not something he was allowed to have. He could see it in others, though, so he knew it was missing—a belief in themselves, rooted in someplace, somebody, a sense of worth they possessed like wealth. Days, he could survive, seeing them all separate, on their way between places, focused on things of little consequence like crossing the street. But nights, nights were harder; he knew they were all gathered together in their rooms. Nights, even the insects communed at the lamps and it was only he that was alone.

This evening, the sun slipped between the buildings for the last time and he understood. The pigeons all returned to the roof edges. The city park quieted, its traffic abating, and it was as if a cloud passed through him that dimmed all things, as if an endpoint had been reached. Now, night is fully here and still he wavers beside his body. After all this, he cannot bear to leave it. It looks so helpless and so wondrous, arrayed there in all that blood.

Prisoners

The girl has grown up beside the prison. She passes the walls every day. She sees the sun gleam on the razor wire and imagines she can feel the massive doors opening and closing beneath her feet. State vehicles often rumble by, rarely with more than momentary faces in windows. Some nights, the girl dreams of an escaped prisoner's hands at her throat. The man wants help evading capture. Food or a weapon. The girl is frightened and runs to tell her parents, but always they lie murdered in their bed. What is she to do now? Alone in this life with a baby brother to protect? The girl readies herself for the worst; the prisoner has followed to brother's room. The girl has her body between the crib and the door. And always, at this dire point she wakes, charged with drama, unable to sleep, her heart having quickened. Tonight, she opens a window to listen. There is a distant siren, but not so much as a tomcat on her neighborhood streets. The wind bristles in the elm trees. She thinks about life behind the walls. What the cells must be like compared to her comfortable bed and her bathroom with a door on it. She thinks about the air hundreds of men have breathed first. What could you call yours in a place like that? How could you stay you? Who wouldn't kill or kidnap a schoolgirl to get out of town? Now, her mother comes in and puts her back to bed, away from the window. A mother just knows. In fact, she has her own unsettling dream of the prisoner, as does the father, as does everyone in the town. Even the prisoner dreams, though he does so of waking up to breakfast with loud children and a demanding wife, then facing a job he isn't trained to do. But soon enough, the dreams will stop. Soon enough, it will be morning again. And only the sun will be vaulting the guard towers, only the birds will be flying to and fro over the imposing prison walls.

Past Loves

All he asks for now is a cup of water to end the evening. Offer him that and he will be on his way. There was a time when wine would have kept the old man here all night. His body was strong enough to bear the mistakes; his life had enough room in which to turn around. In the Stone Age, they must have kept one communal fire always lit and come to it individually for flame. Likewise, the man would have wandered amongst the overturned beer bottles, and the hors d'oeuvre plates flecked with ashes; he would have wound through the wreckage toward one woman or another in hopes of bringing embers back to his cold rooms. All in the name of being loved, of being wanted, of having a stake in the world. Votive candles guttering or burnt out entirely; the looped playlist a painfully transparent vehicle of desire; a few scattered couples and hopeful stragglers who have yet to gather their belongings; the night air sultry, the patio dim, constellations of city lights extinguished and birthed as far as one can see—yes, there was a time he would have stayed, as if to claim his place in time.

It is enough now to look at those lights, then walk the streets and let the wash of youth engulf him as he passes. Nights like this, he recalls women he met in such ways, he sees them as clearly as memory will allow, and they stroll. There have not been very many women in his life. He can remember each and every one. He pretends to know something of the lives they led beyond him, the families they had, the burdens they carried. He imagines them having aged now, gray at the temples, their faces flaccid, their bodies misshapen like his. He asks after their husbands or, in one case, wife; he pretends they are having coffee on an ordinary afternoon. Sometimes when he seems to others to be an old fool talking to himself, he is really with one of them, celebrating a birthday or some feigned good news. . . .

Knowledge of the present, the truth, is not the point. Most he could not find, some, he knows have passed from this life, still others would not want to hear from him, even today. The point is they knew him in ways that no family member could and took part in moments no friend can share. This mattered once and that, he thinks, is enough to matter always. Once you have been loved, you are never again alone.

Ladder on the Ground

I am painting my house for the third and last time. Before this weathers, I will be in an apartment or in the earth. There comes a day, as my granddad warned, when the field is too long to plow. You have a way of life, but can't do it justice. All the chores that defined you as a father and husband, all the sheer sweat labor of maintaining a home, all the tools you accrued, the knowledge—every bit is unnecessary.

There were harbingers. The family vacation was an early casualty. The road trips, the unforced togetherness, the frustrations and joys of being cramped in a car with testy tempers and low blood sugars, but bound for some common experience—suddenly, you actually arrive at an end. The children age; they'd rather be with friends. Soon, it barely matters if you decorate for holidays or nest fresh flowers near the door. You can feel in some cluttered hall closet of your psyche, a need to divest yourself of the extraneous, but what is that exactly? What stays and what goes, what is you and what is not? And how is it one knows?

Lately, watching movies, I pay more attention to extras than the leads. Even during the climactic scenes, I watch the surrounding faces and gestures. Such interest isn't technical, though it is, I suppose, about how such moments are composed. The background detail—the portraits on the wall, book titles stacked beside the bed, the people queued behind in the checkout lane—they are what move me. All these lives alongside others, lived *within*. In the end, we mostly exist behind the scenes. Who am I, now that there is less to provide?

I will miss ladders. Or should I say, I will miss my expertise with them, on them. When I finish, when I rest this one on its side, on the ground, I will even throw a little wrap party. Just me and a cold beer in the garage, I guess, but hey, the big stars never come to these things.

I Love You, Boy

At ninety, my father has one last lesson for me. It is called dying and he has decided, without saying such, to show me how it's done. Once a man of few words, and those about politics or modern values, now, when every sentence could be his last, he has renounced petty wisdom in favor of daily reports. No complaints, no dire predictions, just his pills and supplements, the windshield wiper change, keeping bird seed in the feeders, which once only mother cared about, but of late, he maintains.

He is fortunate, I know, healthy enough to get around, still *himself,* as we say—no dementia, no sudden certainty his children were fathered by his best friend. No, in fact he could not be further away from rage, be that against others or against the dying of the light. Here, at the end of day, my father is teaching me how to be a man, to stand as tall as you still can and walk right through the door under your own power, to saunter toward the inevitable with neither bang nor whimper.

No matter if the squirrels and sparrows are fighting it out again. His papers are in order, his wife's annuity in force, his children and grandchildren (mostly) back in the fold. There's pattern where need be—applesauce helps with larger pills—but there's the spontaneous drive after a single pear. And as for his tinkering in the garage, my mother claims not to know what goes on down there. He oils his tools, dilutes antifreeze; he sorts loose parts, keeps what he needs. No sense now to fashion newer ones—use your time wisely, make sure what's done stays done. Initiate the phone calls. Say you love your son.

The lesson's more what we do, though, than what we say. And I think I'd like to live this way—each morning a gift one wakes to, a scattering of seeds under the trees, simple chores. And don't you worry about the birds—no matter that the squirrels eat most of it, we'll just put out more.

The Journey to and from Is Neither

It is trying, my father says, to watch one's friends wear out. The bodies giving up less to disease or accident now, and more to common use. By this, he means his peers, a diminishment that is ongoing and relentless. The joints won't sustain the pressures, the heart can't pump as much blood, poor hearing and sight restrict most acts. Each milestone is a new need for help, the assistance required for once mundane tasks—getting out of the pool, say, or a lounge chair, perhaps even shoes to be tied. There is something vulnerable and exposed about how it feels, he says. You come out of the barbershop, for instance, and suddenly sense the wind on the back of your neck, the way you did as a boy. Or perhaps it is like when you first kissed a girl in front of her father. There is something you have done that you cannot take back and perhaps cannot atone for and most certainly can never accomplish again.

Those sedate morning strolls? You can no longer take them, even with a cane, your feet now swollen and misshapen by your weight. Those feet that have carried you tens of thousands of miles—door to door, nation to nation, toward marriage, parenthood and patriarchy—and have now brought you to breakfast at Denny's and deposited you firmly in the glacial remains of your time on earth. In fact, most movement is difficult, my father says. It is as if you suddenly can't pull the oar from the river, it is stuck there like a silk fern in a vase watered with hardened acrylic. Eating, conversing, figuring the bill—you can see it on their faces, the effort expended, the frustrating failures of muscle memory and dexterity. You can see it in how they cock their heads, as if catching the tune of an ice cream truck, dim, a neighborhood away, the childish piping of "Turkey in the Straw" and it never dissipates or comes closer, does it, it is always vaguely there, like the voices of parents that can still be heard berating or praising, it no longer matters which now, the point is that they are still speaking inside one, still scuffling on their own frail feet from room to room in the soul.

Have we come at a bad time? More likely than not. That's just how it is. My father's friend, George, barely has the strength to smile, thin as he has become, eroded by the intimacies of time, the strokings of age, the kisses of finality. I was at his home, surrounded by family, in 1969 when Armstrong stepped onto the moon. But leaving a legacy, be it a family or work or some seemingly immortal feat, these put off the inevitable by a few years at most. Ultimately, we become mere names, words, and then are gone into the air like the scent of something almost recognized, but dispersed by wind. It is simple physics: an action here, its equal and opposite reaction there. In the end, there is only energy, positive or negative, momentum that carries forward for better or for ill. You hope to have done your adequate part. You hope to be genuinely mourned and missed. You hope the world is no poorer for your having lived.

The Edge

It is Florida, August 1963, my grandfather's arms are thin and sharp-boned, he is closer to seventy than sixty. My mother is thirty-eight, beautiful, still bearing weight from giving birth to my brother; she will try, but never shed it. They are walking beside each other. She has flowers on her swimsuit and he has parrots on his; he is gazing toward the surf, she peers down and away, as if scanning for shells. Neither seems to know that I am there, let alone that I will be here now, watching them pause forever, poised mid-step between this and then, as if they could stride from the gleaming beach right into my study, to confront me, to ask what exactly it is I have made of the life they had such high hopes for.

And me, what beckons me to the brink of nostalgia, keeps me at the edges of the past, still a seven-year-old boy with a brownie camera to one eye, taking this picture, recording just how bright and strange the world was, a land of glare and long-shadowed contrasts, the ocean vast and indifferent, the sea winds smelling of the small deaths all around us? What is it that has drawn me back, now sixty myself, to these old slides, grainy with age and blurred from scanning, so that in these dim, early hours I pore over that vacation as if for some long-hidden clue, some message that at last, at this late juncture, might tell me who I am and how to approach what remains of my days. I see his ribs below his flaccid breasts, I see the clavicle below his throat—I know what he is now, posed in his grave, his Sunday clothes in tatters. What is it he might say to me, were he to look up, away from the empty horizon and toward me?

Such a cliché, to arrive at this phase, to find yourself foreseeing a parent's funeral and forced to question your life. But then, as a student once reminded me, it is not a cliché when it is happening to you for the first time, nor is it just your turn—it is the first and only end of the first and only world, and we bear it alone, as if unseen by those around us, having to now let go of the hands we held as children, the hands that stroked our hair, or put cool palms to our foreheads—having to watch them pass from our lives, seamlessly as a slideshow slipping from one decade into the next, their jewelry, tools, utensils all that's left to mark the space they inhabited. We take brief ownership of such things; we snap our photos, we make our plans. World within world within world, yet still we arrive at ourselves. And we living are, I know, supposed to move on. But this morning, it is clearly I who am paused, I who am suspended; I'm the one who's wading at the edge of the water.

The Late Show

This loneliness is decades deep and cannot be filled by the descending snow. Nor by the few cars that seem to move through it, but are only projected on yet another screen, a smaller set, between the sound stage's hollow lampposts and phone poles, easily nestled around the Christmas shop windows.

Sixty years ago, you could yell *cut* and the snow would stop immediately, thirty men and women converging in the frame to manage and maintain the last moment filmed. Amalgamations of light, enactments of form and idea, the disembodied façade of human interactions—sixty years ago, these gestures were made, these sounds uttered, flashbacks staged and grafted on. The actor and actress who pretend to love each other did not speak all day, beyond their lines, preoccupied, as they were, with their own dramas—kids ill at home, a bear market, affairs of the heart. And many, many times, the story stalled and started due to faulty equipment and technical error.

Yet still the tale is told, fixed now for eternity, spooled in its reel of moments, and still we are moved to anguish or laughter by actions that never really happened, by realities without context or physical being, at all. Since 1954, the snow has fallen, yet there's a mere dusting on the wintry streets. And just so, film after film, our theater screens never fill: layer upon layer, they remain blank as ever, untouched, unencumbered, ready to begin.

Special thanks to David Jauss for his help with this manuscript and to Clint McCown for his support of it. I am also grateful to David Rivard and Cynthia Huntington for their readings of earlier versions. To my partner, Nancy Card: thank you for buoying my spirit every day.

Some of these poems were written during a research reassignment generously provided by the University of North Carolina Wilmington, for which I am duly appreciative.

Mark Cox has previously published four books of poetry, most recently, *Sorrow Bread, New and Selected Poems: 1984-2015* (Serving House Books), and *Natural Causes* (Pitt Poetry Series, 2004). The recipient of a Whiting Writers Award, a Pushcart Prize, and numerous fellowships for his work, he teaches at the University of North Carolina Wilmington and in the Vermont College MFA Program.

CPSIA information can be obtained
at www.ICGtesting.com
Printed in the USA
BVOW09s0542260218
509030BV00001B/103/P